MAKING YOUR OWN JUMPS

Illustrations by
Carole Vincer

KENILWORTH PRESS

First published in Great Britain by
The Kenilworth Press Limited,
Addington, Buckingham, MK18 2JR

© The Kenilworth Press Limited 1988
Reprinted 1990 (twice), 1992 (twice), 1993,
1994, 1995, 1997
Revised 1999

British Library Cataloguing in Publication Data
A catalogue record for this book is available from the British Library.

ISBN 1-901366-76-5

Printed in Great Britain by Westway Offset, Wembley

CONTENTS

Introduction

Jumping is fun. Most horses or ponies will jump small obstacles happily, but if a horse is unwilling to jump, or is too excited or nervous to jump safely, it ceases to be fun. When bad jumping is caused by bad riding, or by poor training, some helpful instruction can put it right. But far too often it is uninviting, poorly designed and badly built fences which put horses off jumping – sometimes for ever. Even a well-built obstacle can be dangerous in the wrong place.

Making a fence is not just a matter of carpentry. It has to be planned and sited carefully, according to the area available, the conditions, and the standard of those who will be jumping it. All horses need to practise and 'warm up' over something easy, before attempting more challenging or complicated obstacles. Basic knowledge of fence building, common sense, and a little imagination are all useful assets.

A well-designed, solid, and durable jump need not be particularly elaborate or expensive to make, and it can give many years of pleasure. It will also encourage better jumping and cut down the risks of accident and injury.

The practice field

The size of a jumping practice area is less important than its ground conditions ('going'). One or two obstacles in a small space – a maximum of 130ft x 65ft (40m x 20m) – and on a good, well-drained surface, is better than lots of fences in a large field that is too rough, or too deep, or too hard, or boggy, or slippery.

Conditions are rarely ideal, so make the most of the area available: fill the holes, improve the drainage, add gravel, sand or shavings where necessary.

Fences designed to be jumped in both directions are especially useful when space is limited. If three jumps can become six they make a course. A smart set of expensive show jumps is unnecessary, but you do need poles,

with posts or wings and cups to rest them on.

Horses have more respect for solid-looking jumps than weak, flimsy ones which will scatter, break and need constant re-building. Well-made jumps will also last much longer.

Portable jumps can be moved around, giving variety, but they should look solid and not tip over easily. Always leave enough space for a straight approach and a smooth route to the next fence.

Any natural features can be used to design interesting cross-country-type fences, like ditches, slopes, and dips. If you plan a course of fences, a suitable order might be: small – smallish – bigger – big and testing.

Show jump stands, wings and cups

Safety is the most important factor in the design of show jumping. To avoid injury to horse or rider, every part of a show jump must fall down on impact.

Jump cups vary in depth, but a thin pole in a deep cup (2ins or 5cm) is difficult to dislodge and might cause a horse to fall. Metal or plastic jump cups can be bought from suppliers of show jumping equipment or metal ones can be made to order by a blacksmith. Remember: they must fit your wings, which often vary considerably in shape, size and design. You can make your own if you have the skill and the appropriate materials.

There must be *no sharp edges or points* on cups, or any other parts of the jump.

A pair of high stands, or wings, at either end, 'frame' a jump, making it more inviting. The stands also support the poles, and fillers.

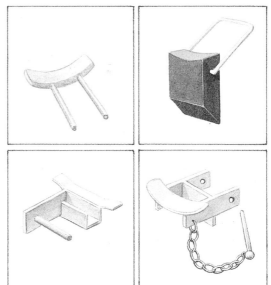

Cups should be 4½–5ins (11–13cm) across and 1½ins (4cm) deep for poles of 4ins (10cm) in diameter. The shape and depth allow a pole to fall more – or less – easily.

Jump wings/stands need feet to keep them stable and upright. Any gaps between slats should be less than 4ins (10cm) or wider than 8ins (20cm), so as not to trap a horse's foot.

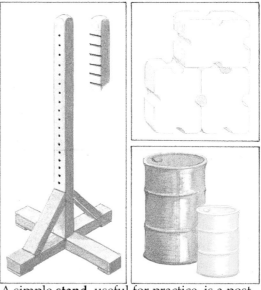

A simple **stand,** useful for practice, is a post set on cross feet, with cup holes drilled 2-4ins (5-10cm) apart. **Plastic blocks** are light and easy to adjust. **Barrels** are useful if stable and not rusty or jagged.

Show jump parts

Show jumps are more interesting if they have variety.

'Fillers' are useful to fill groundline space below top poles, and they give a jump a more solid, inviting appearance than just a few widely spaced poles. They can be painted brightly, or given a 'spooky' design. Wings, jump poles, planks, walls, and most fillers are mostly made of wood, but plastic versions are also available now. Pressure-treated softwood is expensive but lasts longer than untreated woods which rot, splinter, or break easily.

Natural plantation poles will probably taper a little but they are suitable for schooling: the bark should be removed so that a preservative can be applied. All jump parts need maintenance if you want them to last. Paint will help to protect them: use semi-gloss – it does not glare in the sun, and dries quickly.

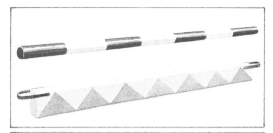

Poles are usually 12 ft (3.5 m) long, 4 ins (10 cm) in diameter. Treated wood is recommended. **Planks** need metal handles to balance on flat cups. They are about 12 ins (30 cm) deep.

Fillers are mostly 2 ft (61 cm) high and must be at least ½ in (1.25 cm) thick, otherwise they might break. They may be in two halves, so that they can be moved. 'Hanging' **panels** need strong handles.

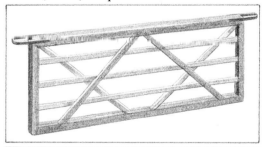

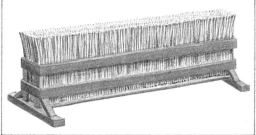

A **gate** can be any height. The projecting handles rest on flat cups so that it can fall freely. Make sure that there is a safe distance between bars. **Brush** packed into a frame makes a good filler but often needs renewing.

Types of show jump

The two basic types of show jump are:

Uprights: Vertical poles, planks, wall, gate.

Spreads: Either sloping, like a triple bar or an oxer; or parallel, like a 'square' oxer, when the front pole is as high as the back (this is more difficult).

Spreads need two pairs of wings, or three pairs for a triple bar. Some uprights, such as a wall, gate, or plank, are the same shape on both sides, so they can usefully be jumped in either direction.

A pole or filler at the base of the jump gives it a 'groundline', which helps a horse to judge his take-off. The upper face of the jump should never be more prominent than any lower part.

Triples, oxers, and parallels, are designed to be jumped in one direction only, *never* in reverse because the 'false' groundline could be disastrous.

Upright poles

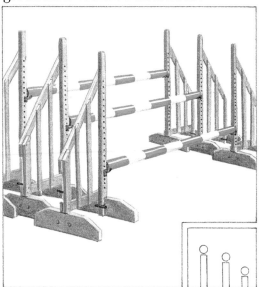

Triple bar

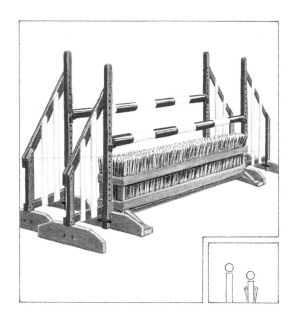

Oxer

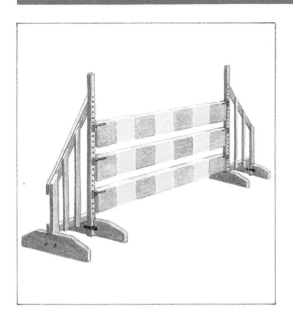

Planks

Wall

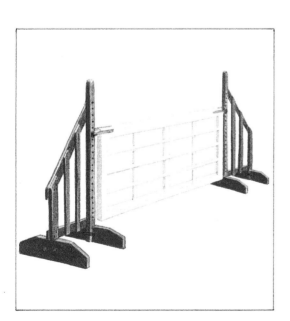

Gate

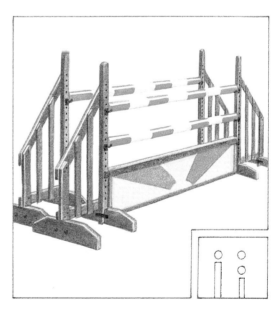

Parallel

Show jump combinations

When two jumps are placed close together they make a **combination**, or **double**. Three jumps in succession form a **treble**.

Combinations have either one, or two, 'non-jumping strides' between elements. A two-stride double is easier because it allows more time to recover from a mistake at the first part. A sloping first element is more inviting than an upright, while a wide spread as a second element is not suitable for horses of limited ability or experience.

Distances between elements must be correct, and are generally based on multiples of 12ft (3.5m), the average length of a horse's canter stride. The distance will be shorter if the jumps are low (less than 3ft/90cm) or for short-striding ponies. The going and gradients must also be considered.

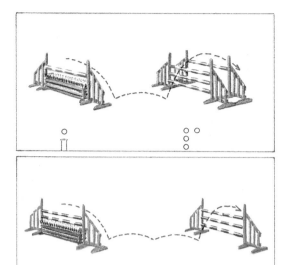

Doubles – one stride
two strides

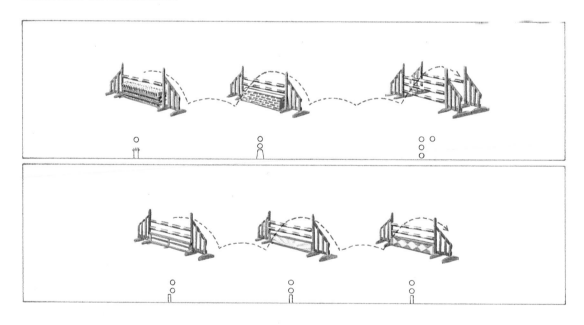

Trebles – one strides and two strides
one stride and one stride

A flimsy-looking jump with airy gaps between thin poles will not be respected by a horse. Poles should be at least 3½ ins (9cm) thick. Any jump with no groundline is also a potential danger.

Use only one top pole on the back wings of a spread, and never a plank or gate. Never leave cups on wings unless they are in use.

Wrong, or trick, distances between combination elements will force a horse to make a mistake, or to perform contortions which are unfair.

Avoid: jumps facing into bright sunlight; dark, confusing shadows: difficult approach and take-off areas (boggy, rough, sloping ground); ill-defined obstacles; jumps that are too high or wide; difficult angles; badly sited jumps, e.g. facing towards a wire fence or trees.

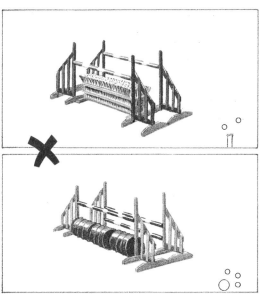

False groundline. The top pole is prominent. *Cans must be fixed*, and the far pole *must* be higher than the front top pole, and clearly visible to a horse *before* take-off. The lower back pole is unnecessary and hazardous.

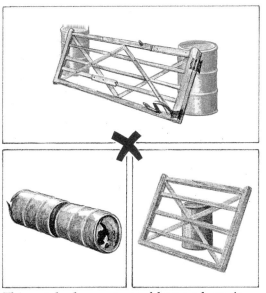

This **patched-up** gate could trap a horse's leg, and cause an injury if he raps it. These **rusty old oil-drums** are not fixed and have jagged edges. The **narrow gate** will teach a horse bad habits, such as running out.

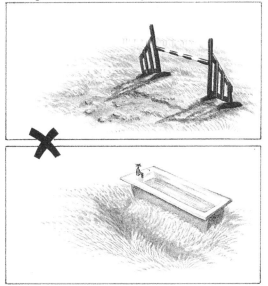

(top) A single pole without a groundline is difficult to judge, or to approach evenly on bumpy ground. *(bottom)* An obstacle with sharp edges, prominent at the top, giving it a false groundline.

Example of a show jumping course plan

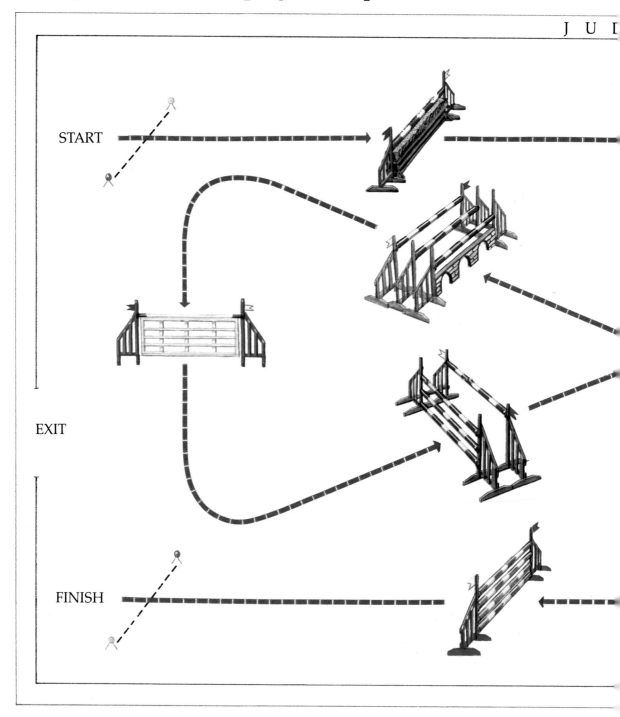

START

EXIT

FINISH

ENTRANCE

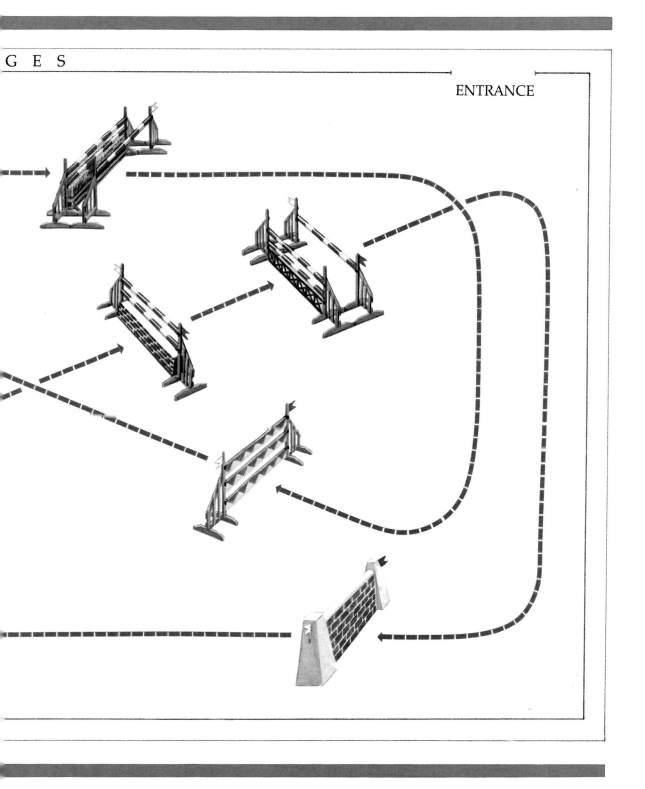

Cross-country fence materials

Most cross-country obstacles are made of timber. This must be strong to withstand countless knocks. Economy will not pay: spindly, weak-looking timber, though cheaper to buy and light to handle, invites careless jumping and soon breaks, whereas a solid fence is safer and lasts much longer.

Horses respect solid-looking tree-trunks, for example, and rarely touch one. Smaller trees or thick branches, about 12ins (30cm) in diameter, make suitable alternatives, but machined poles, from a timber merchant or forester, are easier to work with, to attach to posts, or to alter a height or spread. Telegraph poles are ideal, though heavy to move.

A fence can only be as strong as its posts. Hardwood, chemically treated with a preservative, will last many years; softwood may rot after just a year.

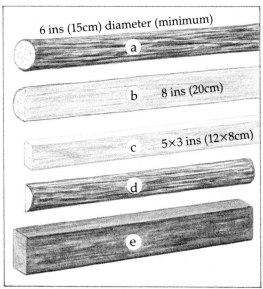

Timber: (a) Round rail (b) Half-round rail (c) Sawn rail (d) Offcut (e) Sleeper
Offcuts are useful fillers, but not strong enough as top rails.
A post is needed at every join.

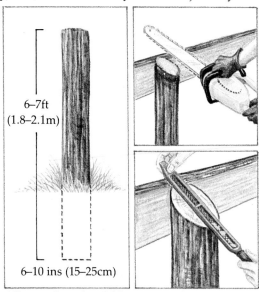

6–7ft
(1.8–2.1m)

6–10 ins (15–25cm)

All uprights should be immovable, with about one third of their total length in the ground. They should not be more than 10 ft (3 m) apart, to support the rails. Ends must be cut off and sharp edges removed.

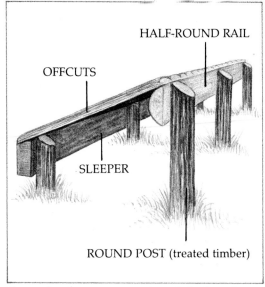

HALF-ROUND RAIL

OFFCUTS

SLEEPER

ROUND POST (treated timber)

Example of a cross-country obstacle using several different types of timber. If creosote or another wood preservative is applied at least once a year, this fence should be 'permanent'.

Cross-country fence construction

A simple, adjustable upright fence can be made by sinking two pairs of stakes or posts 9–12ins (27–36cm) apart, at either end, and drilling pairs of holes at various heights, so that a metal bar can be inserted between the uprights at the chosen level.

To make a spread, poles can be positioned on a horizontal or sloping bar which runs between pairs of stakes about 4ft apart (1.2m). It is then easy to move the pole to make the fence narrower or wider. The poles are kept in place with rope or blocks of wood.

More permanent obstacles may be constructed by fixing rails to posts. Sturdy posts are even more important than the rails they support because they have to withstand most of the impact when struck by a horse at speed.

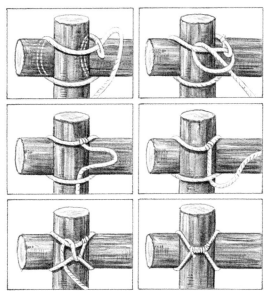

Roping rails to posts is safer than using nails, bolts or wire. Polypropylene ¼in. (6mm) diameter rope does not break, is easy to handle, and can be cut in an emergency. After roping, trim the posts.

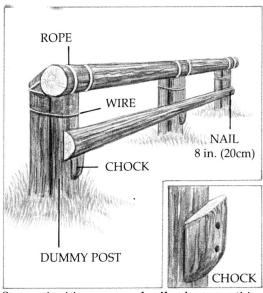

ROPE

WIRE

NAIL
8 in. (20cm)

CHOCK

DUMMY POST

CHOCK

Strong, inviting **post and rails:** the top rail is roped to the main post and supported on an adjustable 'dummy' post. The lower rail, slightly prominent, rests on a chock at one end, for quick release.

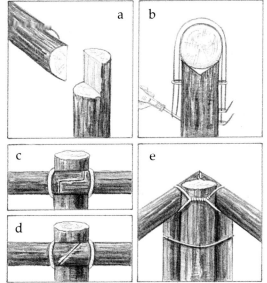

a   b

c

d   e

a Post and rail halved, then roped. **b** Rail notched into top of post, secured with rope, or wire, then stapled to post. **c** Rails halved, and **d** cut diagonally, then butted together. **e** Roping a corner.

Types of cross-country fence

Riding across country over a variety of obstacles and terrain is challenging and exciting. It need not be dangerous.

The difficulty of a fence depends on its dimensions in relation to the abilities of horse and rider, the ground conditions (going), and its actual site. The approach line should be straight and allow a clear view of the obstacle.

A fence must be wide enough – at least 12ft (3.5m). Narrow fences are uninviting, and if horses always take off and land on the same patch of ground, it will become poached and deep, or slippery, hard and bare. A narrow 'island' fence (not in a fenceline) needs **wings** to encourage better jumping. These can be made with brushwood, bales, or rails, and should be higher than the obstacle, to 'frame' it. Trees, bushes, or a safe fenceline (not barbed wire!) can be useful natural wings.

Bales make useful fillers, but must be fixed. A pole above them makes a solid-looking jump. **Parallel** – the back rail must be clearly visible above the top front rail.

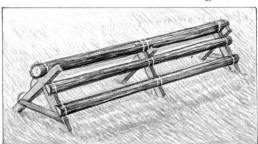

Tiger trap – can be jumped from either side. Beware of narrow gaps that could trap a foot or leg. **Palisade** – could be built as a portable fence, as could the tiger trap, but it must be fixed securely in position.

Cans make good fillers, as long as they are secure and cannot roll around. **Tyres** are versatile as there are many different sizes and possible fence designs. This one is particularly safe and looks inviting.

Triple bar
Bench/seat

Stile
Shark's teeth

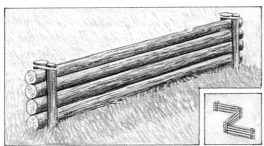

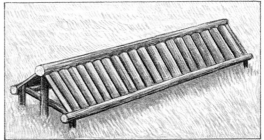

Horizontal rails
Ditch and rails

Hanging log
Coop/pheasant feeder

Some basic cross-country obstacles

Natural fences, like fallen trees or jumpable field boundaries such as rails, hedges, walls, banks, ditches, streams, gates, are not often available as jumps, but similar obstacles can be constructed for schooling at home. Obstacles designed to be jumped from either side are particularly useful. All the fences seen here are 'reversible', *except* the gate and sleeper wall, which both slope away. If jumped in reverse the false groundline would make them dangerous. The frame for the brush fence is made with the front, visible, rail slightly higher than the back rail, which a horse would not see. 'Loose' log piles and cans must be fixed in place: if any part of a jump becomes tangled in the horse's legs, it could bring him down, or at least frighten him. The top rail of a gate usually needs strengthening with an extra pole at the back.

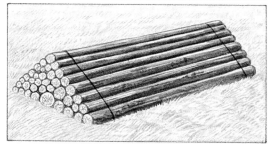

Log piles

Natural hedge
Stone wall, reinforced

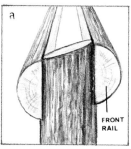

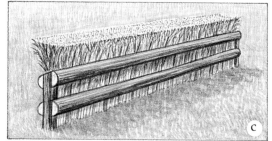

(a) **Brush frame**.　(b) Packing the frame.
(c) **Brush/birch fence**, trimmed.

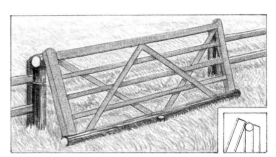

Cans/barrels/oil drums (secured)

Gates, reinforced

Sloping **Sleeper wall**

SAFETY RULES TO REMEMBER

- Any fence with a false groundline (see page 8) is dangerous.

- Sharp edges or protrusions are dangerous on **any** part of a jump.

- Loose materials, e.g. as used in brush or log-pile fences, must be firmly secured.

- Rails must be spaced so that they cannot trap a horse's foot/leg.

- Rope is safer than wire or nails for securing rails since it can easily be cut in an emergency.

- Every fence should be clearly defined so that a horse can see what shape it is before jumping it.

Ditches

A ditch may be jumped on its own or combined with a timber fence, a hedge, or a bank. To be safe, it must have firm, sound, sloping banks. Ditches which are used often will generally need the take-off side reinforced with timber, or *'revetting'*, so that the bank does not break up or become dangerous.

A small, shallow ditch may only need a strong take-off pole, which should be staked in at least 2 ins (5 cm) from the edge of the bank, so that, if the edge wears away, no dangerous gap will appear between the bank and the rail, where a horse's leg might go through. If a ditch has a steep or loose bank, the take-off should be revetted the whole way down. Never revet the landing side: a horse or rider falling against it could be seriously hurt.

Railway sleepers or treated timber are ideal for revetting.

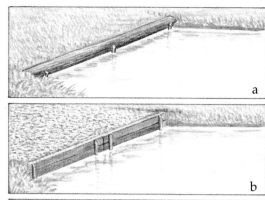

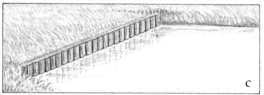

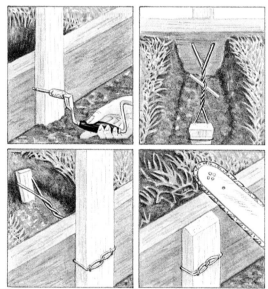

The side of a ditch or bank may be reinforced with
(a) a take-off pole/guard rail, or (b) and (c) revetting: sleepers or treated timber

Preparing the bank, cut to fit the timber. Trenches, opposite outer support stakes, dug back into the bank (about 3½ ft 1 m) for treated stakes to strengthen and hold revetting.

Holes for the wire are bored. Each support stake is wired to its tie-back stake. The wire is stapled then twisted tight. The top timber will be nailed to the stakes, and rough edges trimmed.

Banks and steps

The sides of drops, steps and banks can be reinforced in the same way as a ditch. To contain the pressure of the infilling – and horses jumping – the revetting timbers must be extremely strong, secured with wires attached to vertical posts sunk deep in the ground.

Banks and steps should be revetted on every side, then filled with large hardcore bricks, stones, rubble – and finally topped with layers of finer material, well compressed.

Twist the wire correctly for greater strength.

An upper layer of fine crushed stone or gravel will be added on top of the supporting wires when the final sleepers are in position.

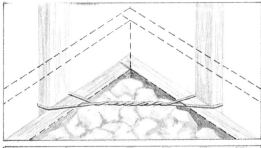

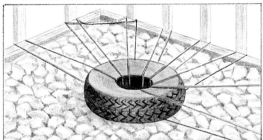

Wiring across a corner between vertical supporting stakes, above the hardcore but below the top sleeper.
Alternative method: using an old tyre.

Revetted steps: this platform is about 18 ft×9 ft (5.5 m×2.5 m). If a bank is sown with grass, or turfed, it will need several months to be safely 'established'.

Cross-country combinations

An obstacle with more than one part, or element, is called a combination. It may be straightforward – such as in and out of a lane or pen; successive steps up or down; or angled rails.

OR it might combine different problems, such as a bank and rail, or a fence followed by a drop, or rail-ditch-rail (coffin).

OR it could offer the rider a choice of route, as with the V-fence which can either be jumped with one stride, no stride (a bounce), or all in one leap over the corner.

- *Never make trick distances*: they can cause a bad accident, especially with fixed fences.
- Always have an 'escape route'.
- Do not ask a horse to jump 'blindly' into a combination.
- Turns within a combination must be smooth, not awkward.

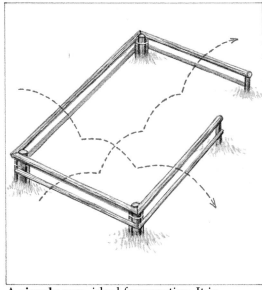

A **simple pen**, ideal for practice. It is designed to be jumped with two strides between elements in one direction, but only one stride from a different approach. Note the 'escape' gap

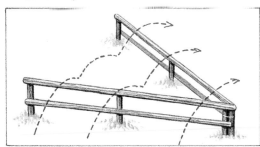

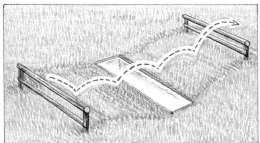

A typical **V-fence**. At their widest point the rails must allow at least one full stride (24 ft/7m). A **coffin** 21 ft (6.4 in) is a suitable distance to allow one stride on both banks. (Both these obstacles could be reversible.)

Angled rails, useful for practising accuracy and obedience. The **two steps up** followed by **rails and a drop**, will test impulsion and boldness. Distances will vary slightly according to fence heights.

Water

To jump *into* water, a horse must trust his rider and his landing must be firm and even. A sound take-off is also vital, whether it is a plain bank (revetted), or over a suitable jump like a log, tyres, or low rail.

Banks which become boggy can be made safe with an artificial surface. A pond or lake which has a soft base should first be drained, and the mud removed and replaced with a firm surface such as hard core and gravel.

IMPORTANT

- A jump OVER water should be less than 10 ft (3 m) across.
- A jump INTO water must be wider than 17 ft (5 m) across.

Any width between these two confuses a horse and is dangerous.

- At least one bank must be sloping for an easy exit.
- The water level needs to be controlled.

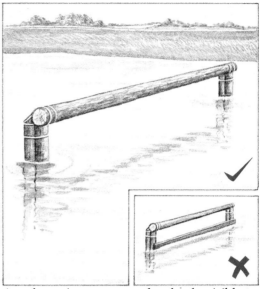

Any fence *in* water must be clearly visible to the horse above the water level. A single suspended pole or log is ideal because the water can wash underneath it and will not splash back against the horse as he takes off.

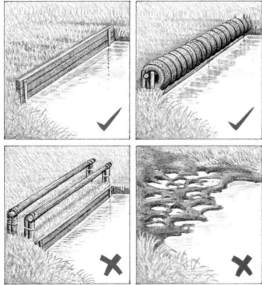

(*Above*) Suitable jumps into water.
(*Below*) Unsuitable. Never build a spread fence into water. A muddy bank pitted with holes will not be trusted by horses.

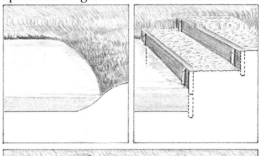

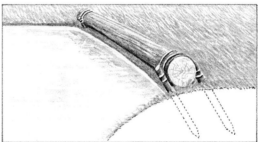

Three sound ways to jump either into water, or out of it. A solid natural bank is ideal but most banks will deteriorate unless they are revetted, or unless a pole or log, as above, is positioned to protect the edge.

Maintenance

Points to remember

- *Show jumps* should be stored under cover in winter, or when not in use.
- Do not leave poles lying in the grass: they will rot, or warp. Always prop up one end so water will run off.
- Keep jump cups dry to avoid rust.
- A fresh coat of paint in summer helps to preserve the wood.
- *Cross-country fences* need creosote or wood preservative every year.
- Check that fence posts have not rotted where they enter the ground.
- A nail in time will save nine.
- A birch fence can be covered with polythene to protect it from livestock, or from becoming brittle when drying out after wet weather.
- Re-turfing, re-seeding, or other earthworks, need several months to 'settle'.
- Water jumps must be drained if the base silts up or if any holes appear

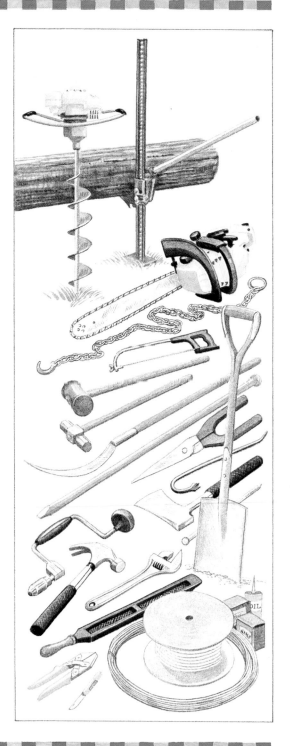

Tools and equipment

A *tractor* or four-wheel drive vehicle will be useful. Major tasks, like digging a ditch or making a bank, require heavy-duty machinery: a tractor mounted with a fore-end loader/bucket/ post-hole borer/post driver; and a tipper, for loads of earth, sand or hardcore. *Post-hole borer* (petrol, or hand version), *high lift jack* (to raise and hold up heavy rails, or pull out posts, with chain attached), *chainsaw* (needs an expert to operate it), *tow chain* (to drag heavy timber), *hacksaw* (D-shaped), *fencing mall/sledgehammer, slasher, crow bar, shears, jemmy, axe, tommy bar, carpenter's brace* (for drilling holes in wood), *claw hammer, adjustable spanner, spade/shovel, surform, pliers, penknife, nails* (4ins/10cm, 5ins/12.5cm, 6ins/15cm), *wire, rope, staples, lubricating oil.*